With gratitude to John Berger for delivering the garden to my cheek

garden on my cheek

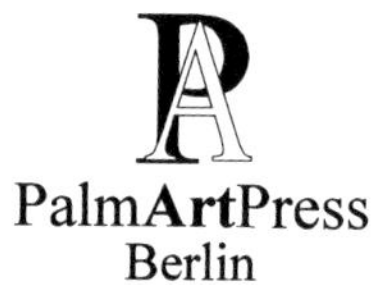

PalmArtPress
Berlin

Das Wort gesetzt als wäre da ein Mund ein Ohr
ein Stift zu hauchen zu fixieren auf Papier
die Schwingungen der Luft dem tauben Ohr vernehmbar
dem blinden Auge oder den Bibliotheken ungefragt
er hätte ja sagen können oder nein es wäre
nichts anders gewesen im Mund im Ohr auf dem Papier
er hätte schweigen können mit seinem Mund seinem Stift
dem Papier etwas verschweigen seinen Mund das Wort
den Stift in der Hand die Hand verschweigen einfach schweigen
und den Stift arbeiten lassen auf gefräßigem Papier

Jürgen Wellbrock

The word is placed as if the mouth were an ear
to breath in a pen and bring it to paper
the vibrations in the air audible for the deaf ear
the blind eye or the librarian unasked
he could have said yes or no it would have
been no different in mouth in ear on to the paper
he could have kept silent with his mouth his pen
to silence something from the paper his mouth the word
the pen in hand the hand is kept silent simply silent
and to let the pen to work on voracious paper

Alpage

Murmuring river
clasps the mist
for a moment more.
The peaks are signing on
the sky.
Stop and hear
the milking machines
designed to suck like calves.
In the first heat
the forested hills calculate
their steepness.
The lorry driver is taking the road
to the pass which leads
surprisingly
with its own familiarity
to another homeland.
Soon the grass will be
warmer
than the cows´ horns.
The astounding comes
towards us
outrider of death and birth.

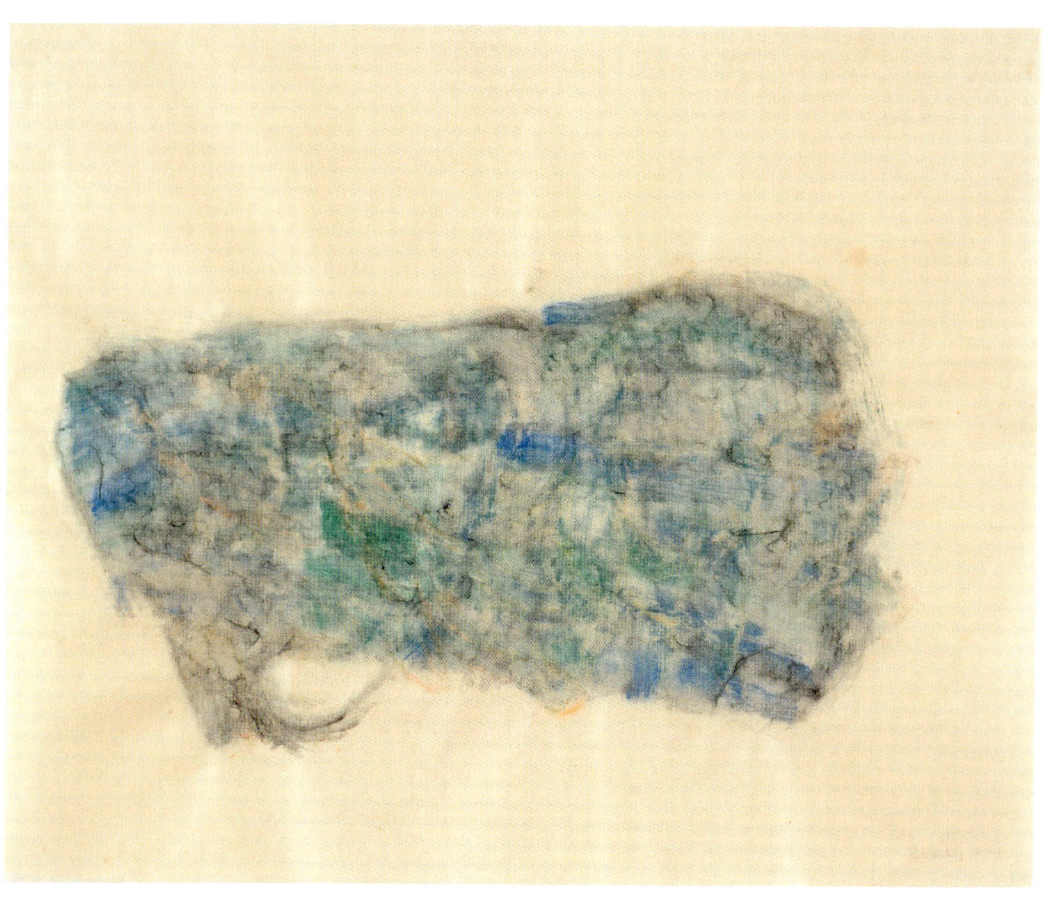

At Remaurian

II

A butterfly disturbs a grain
The grain another
Till there is such friction in the dust
The sky spills its blue milk
On the stones that have conceived

A day is born

Down the precipitous gaze of its opened eyes
The trees are led.

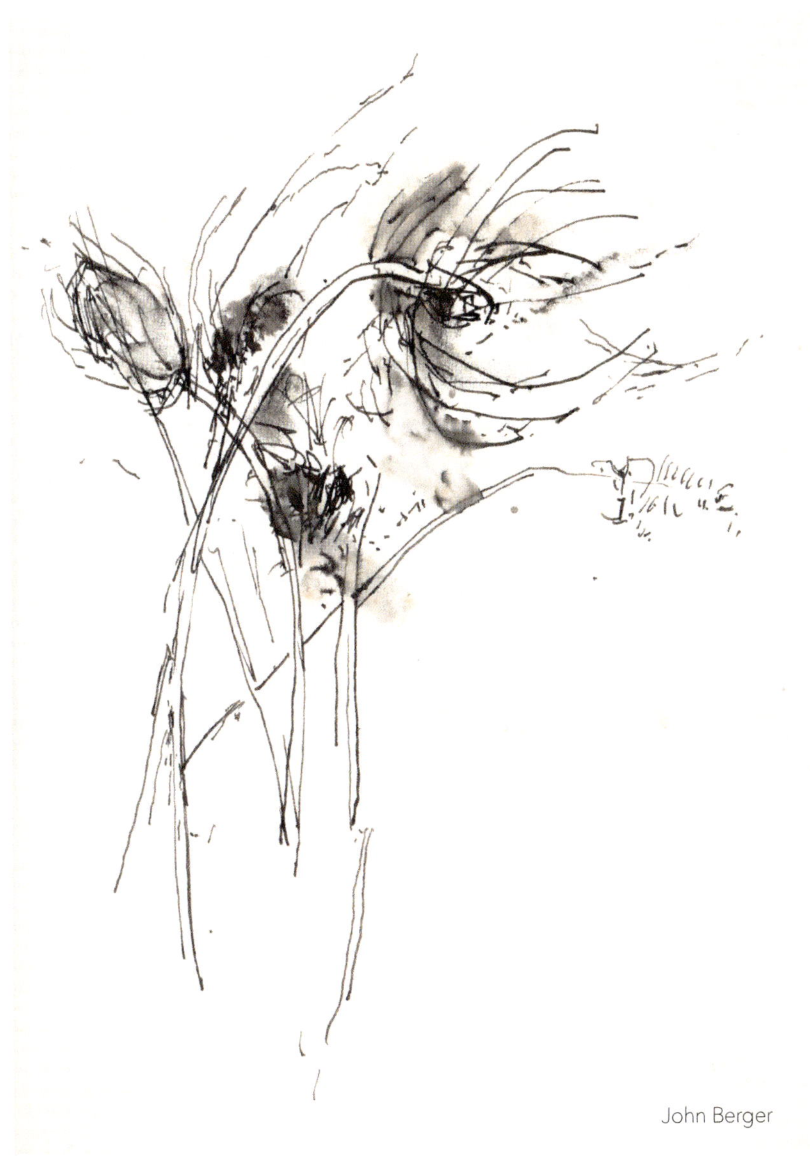

John Berger

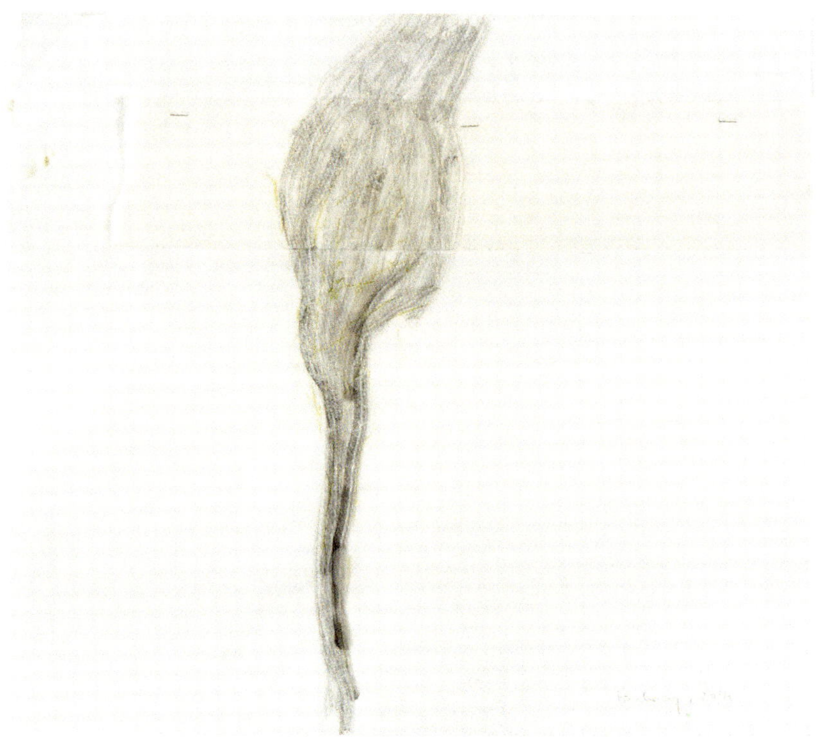

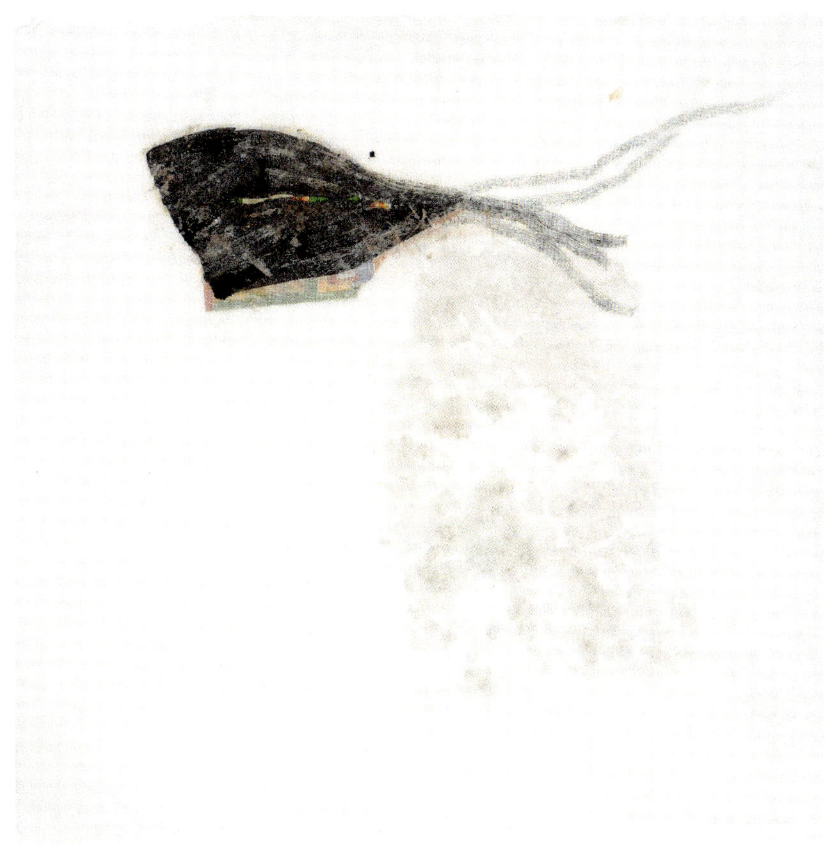

Orchard

On my way to the sea
I passed an orchard

the branches of the trees
exposed to the prevailing
sea wind
were tangled

likewise their shadows

that day there was no wind

the cows in the orchard
twitched their flanks in the sunlight
to disturb the flies

in the tangled shadows daisies
made me imagine
how a grain of sand might open
and white petals radiate
from the opened yellow grain

the late blossom on a tree
at the orchard´s edge
was the colour of my brain
white rose with flecks of light and blood

thoughts in a brain
stay invisible
hence words to reveal.

I thought:
every day this orchard
is part of
          a gale.

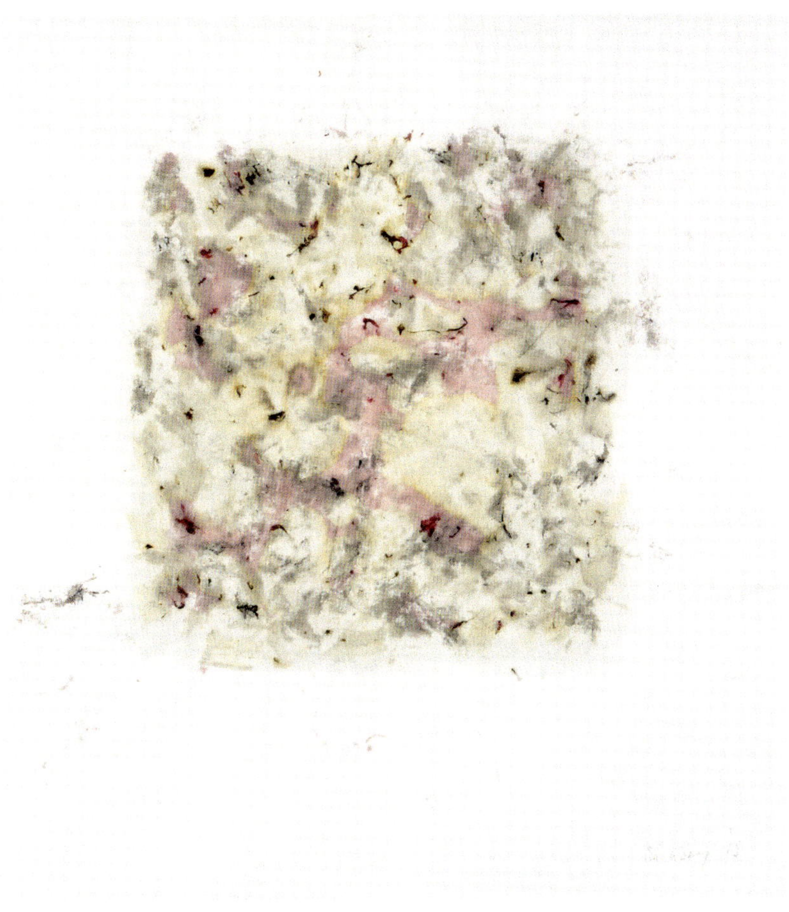

Snow

The covering bird
who came in November
to build a nest
with forests of pine
orchards roofs and fences
is going to vanish.

His white wings lie
discarded
on the green sky
whose stars are crocuses.

Tomorrow
his last seed
will disappear like salt into meat
and soon I'll saw the wood
he broke
when he came to fuck our winter.

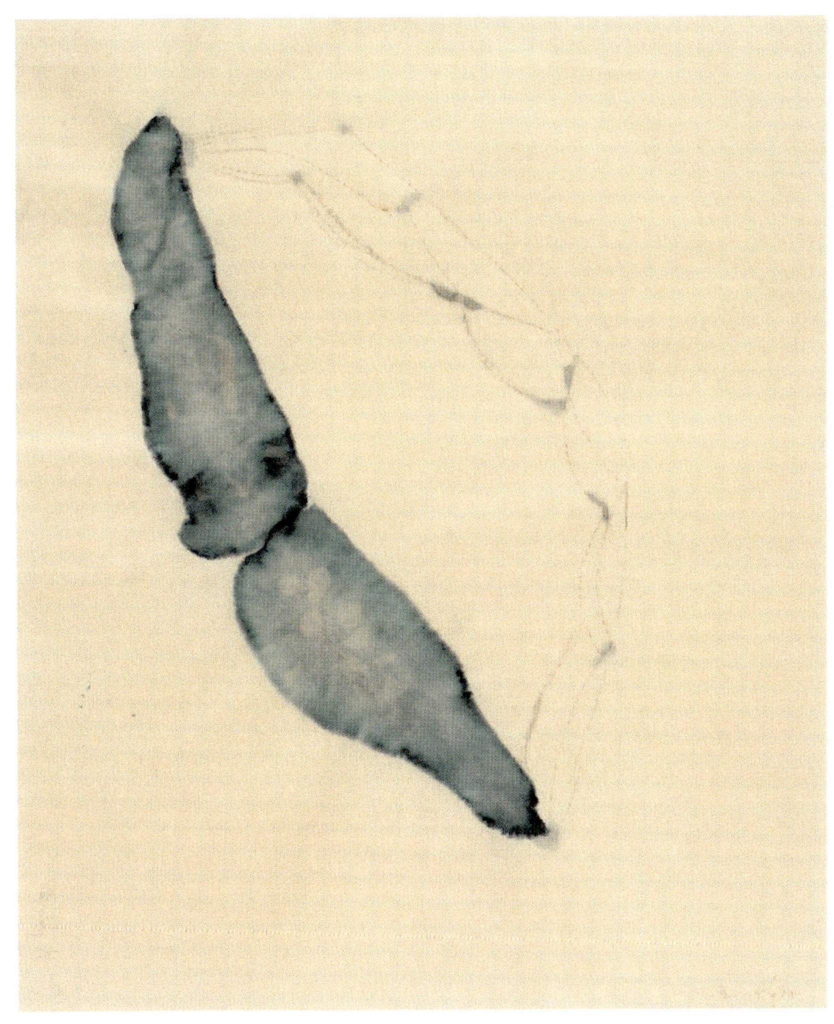

Pages

Word by word I describe
you accept each fact
and ask yourself:
what does he really mean?

Quarto after quarto of sky
salt sky
sky of the placid tear
printed from the other sky
punched with stars
Pages laid out to dry.

Birds like letters fly away
O let us fly away
circle and settle on the water
near the fort of the illegible.

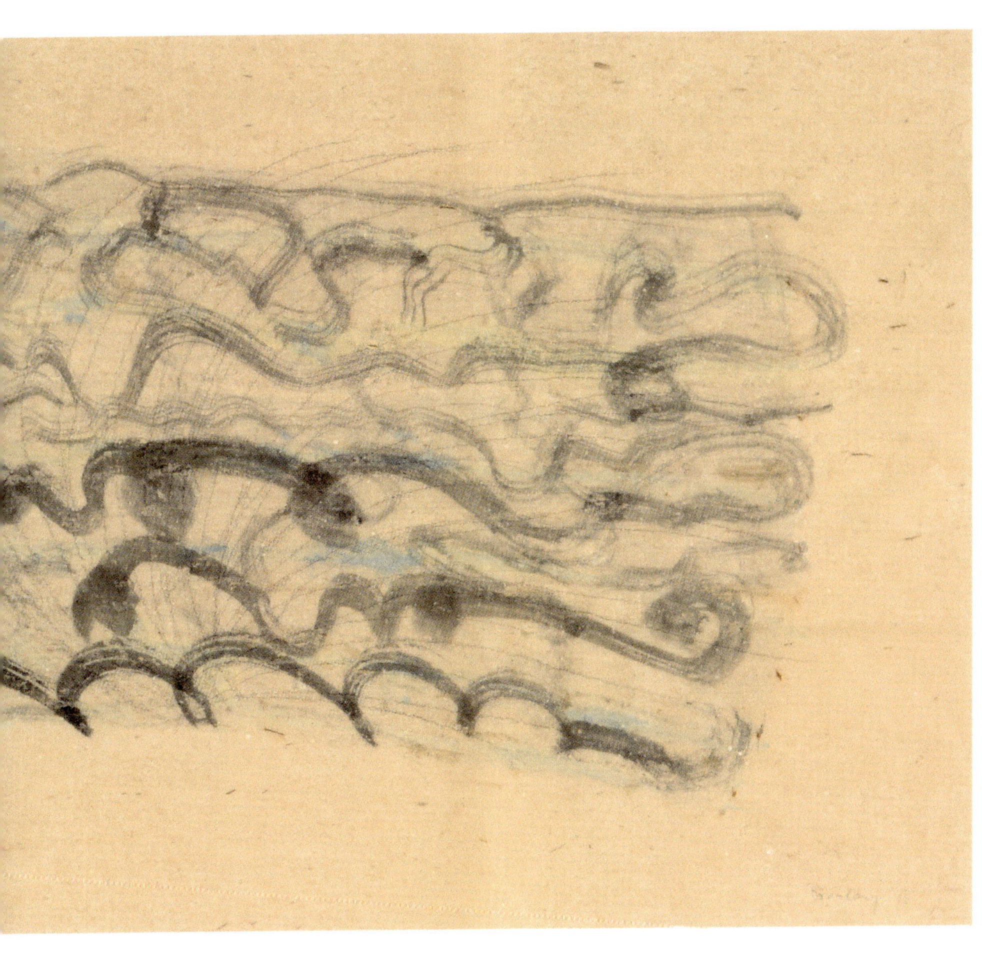

Likeness

Who is drawing me
between pencil and paper?

One day I shall judge the likeness
but she who judges
will not be the woman who now
so expectantly poses.

I am what I am.

What I am like is how you see me.

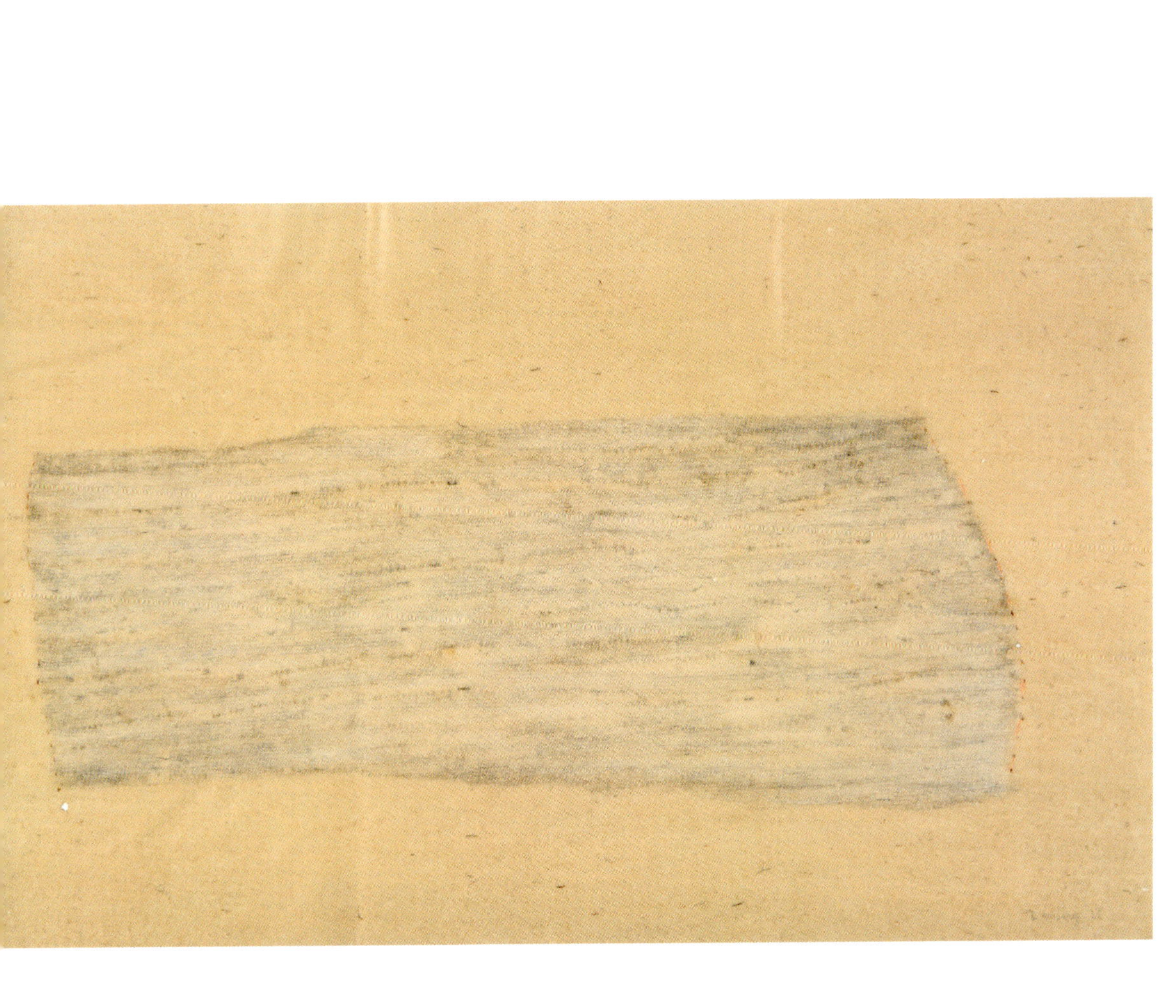

The Unsaid

On my table
a pile of letters
not yet replied to
the earliest dated
three years before.
One evening I decide
the time has come
to deal with them all.
Letters from poets
more lyrical than I
requesting advice,
letters from institutions
inviting me to speak
on communication
or the use of art...
from an insurance company
a reminder explaining
I had overlooked
the obligatory premium
against natural disasters,
a birthday card.

Among the post unanswered
two letters
from close friends.
The handwritings,
one fat and one thin,
not easy to decipher,
yet over the years
I had read them avidly
finding encouragement.

Now both are dead
their last letters
lost in a pile:
both killed themselves
one with a gun
one in a canal.

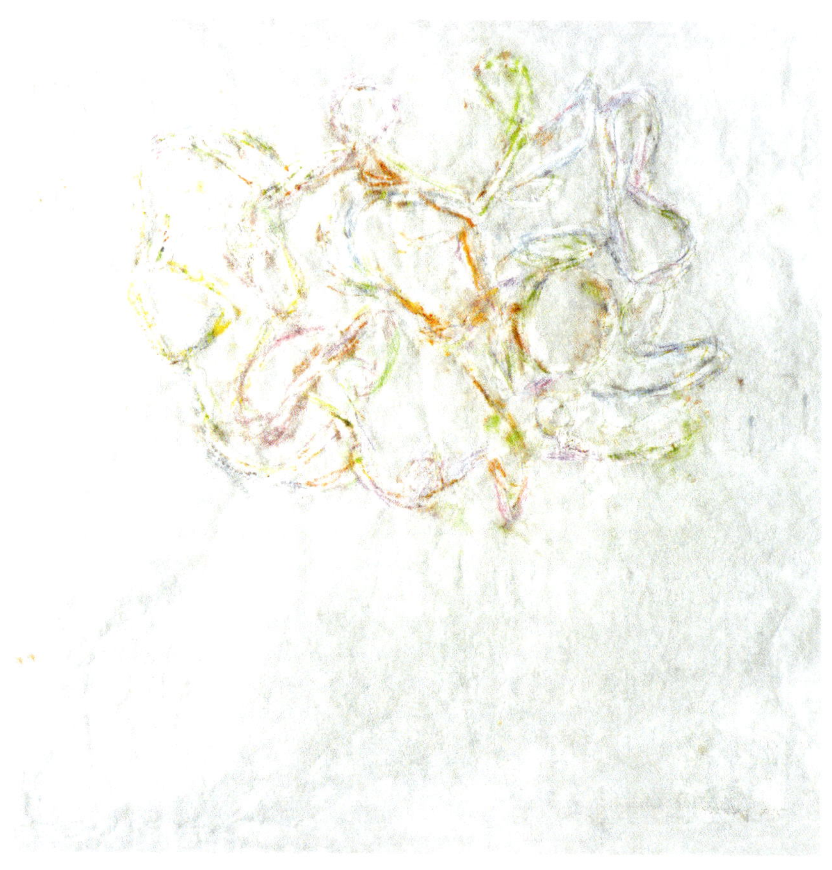

Family Tree

You have unusually long arms
said the salesman
glad of the chance to use
fitting critical criteria
when I went to buy my coat.

Your arches are unusually high
said the woman
forty years ago
who came each week
to set my mother's hair
and knew a little chiropody.

An unusually strong jaw yours
said the Austrian dentist when
head back and mouth open
I let him extract a tooth
in North London.

Soon such attributes will be as
indistinguishable as particles
in the cloud of white dust
which settles on the grass
when the cart has passed
            cows grass
            grass of the neighbour's horse
            two sheeps grass
            fowls grass
            grass of four apple trees
            Serbian grass
            my ancestors scythed.

I have unusually long arms
their length
would have made scything easier.

At Remaurian

III

At the nocturnal level of the hand
Herbs must always grow
Leaf of my leaf
But early enough
And upright
Following in the wake of the trees
I have felt against the vein of my wrist
Webs breaking
Till every connection of the night is severed
And single I step forward to become
The honey-coloured fleck
On the iris of the first comer´s eye.

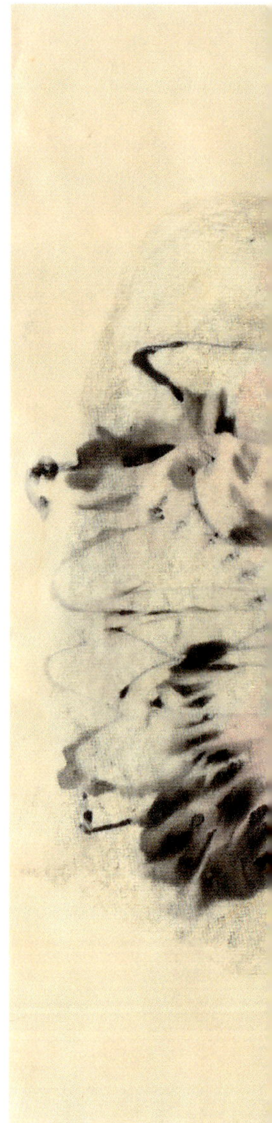

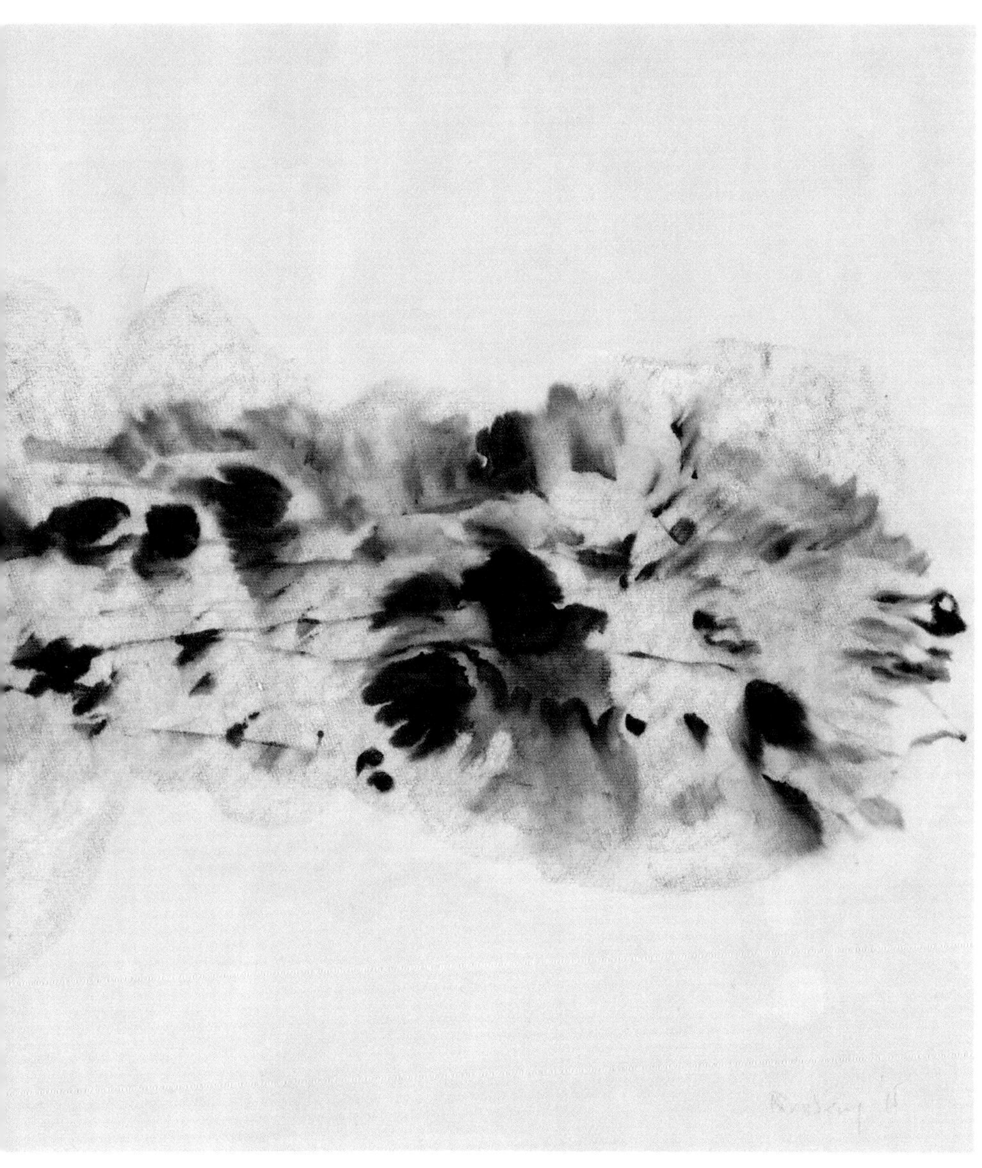

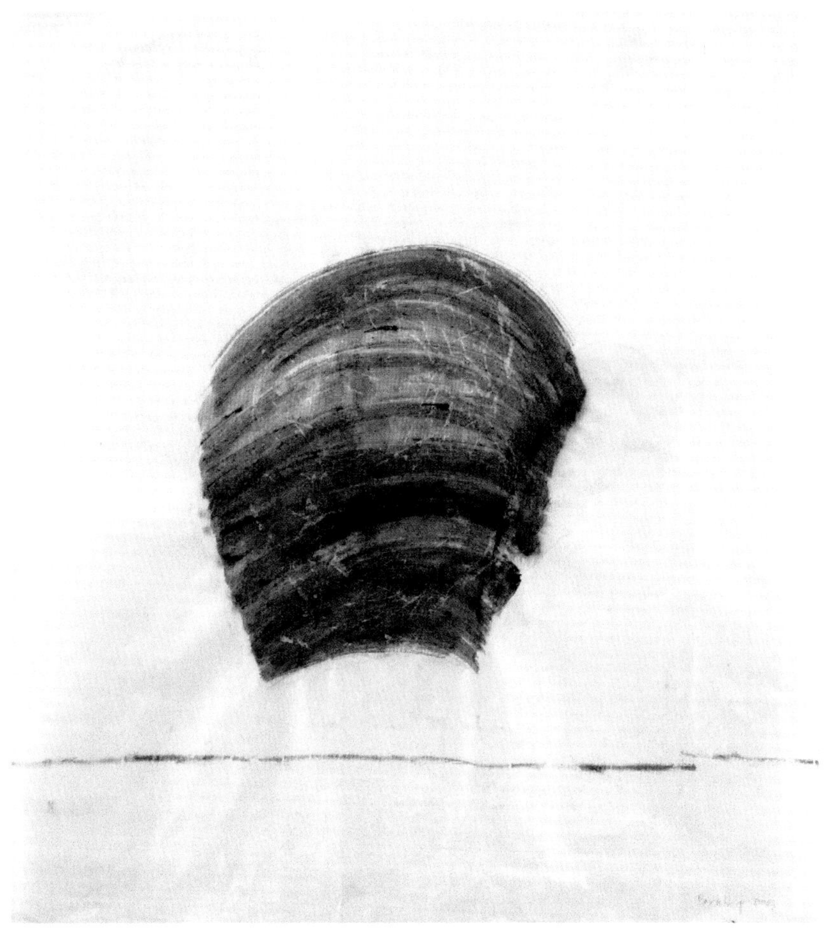

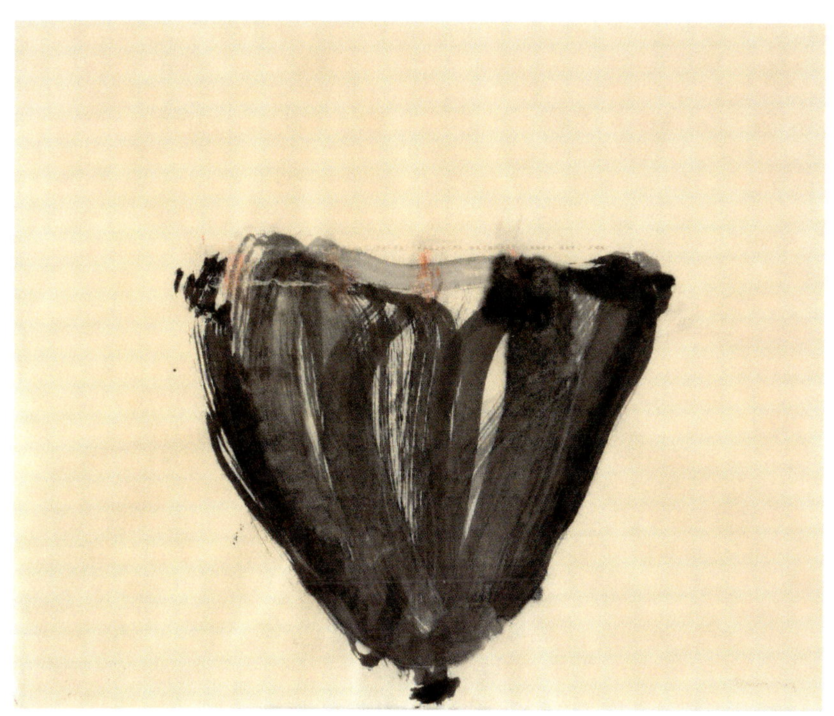

My Honey

The apple trees are barking
the beestings on my scalp
mark the rage of the swarm
hold, my honey, your sweetness.

The sky is pressing its thumbs
into my eyes
his constellations are fleeing
hold, my honey, your sweetness.

The endless rain
desiring the mountains as sand
is preparing me for bed
hold, my honey, your sweetness.

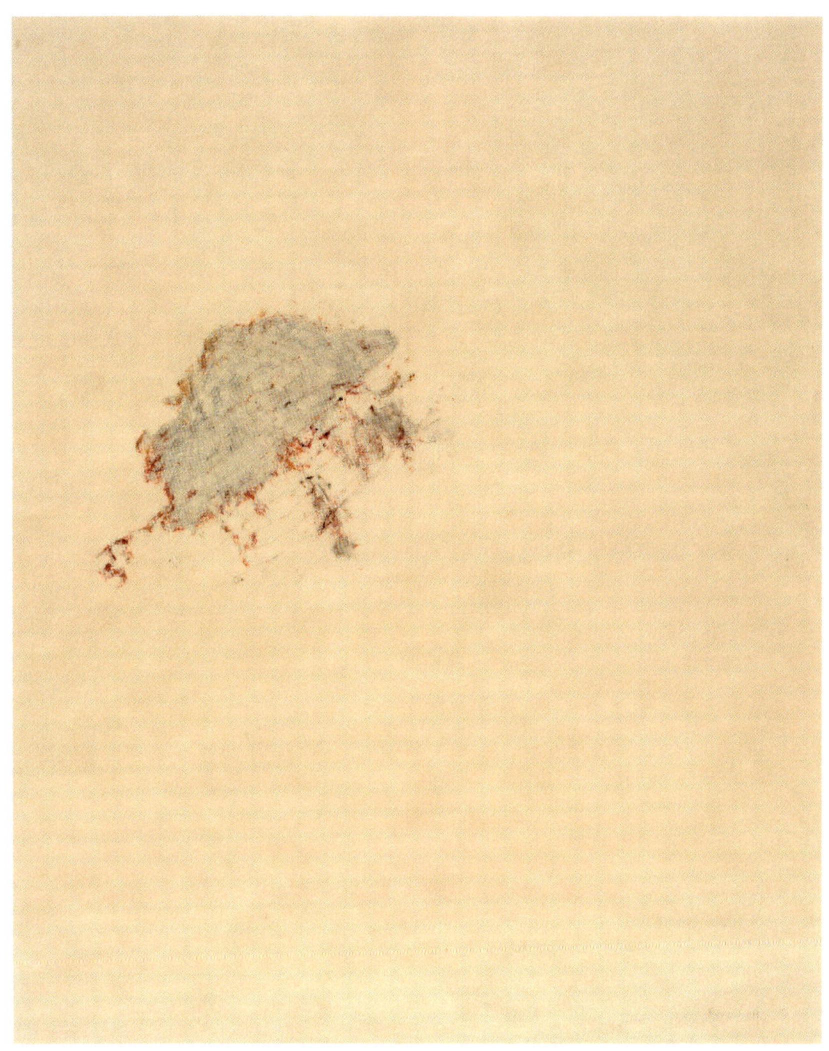

Lovers in a Park

The magnolia is in flower

In the old conservatory
        pensioners are playing cards

The magnolia is in flower

A gardener drives a rotary mower
        without its blades

The magnolia is in flower

Blowing last years leaves
        from the flowering beds

The magnolia is in flower

To lift me from the earth
        place your hands far below

The magnolia is in flower

So that my roots come away
        with their soil.

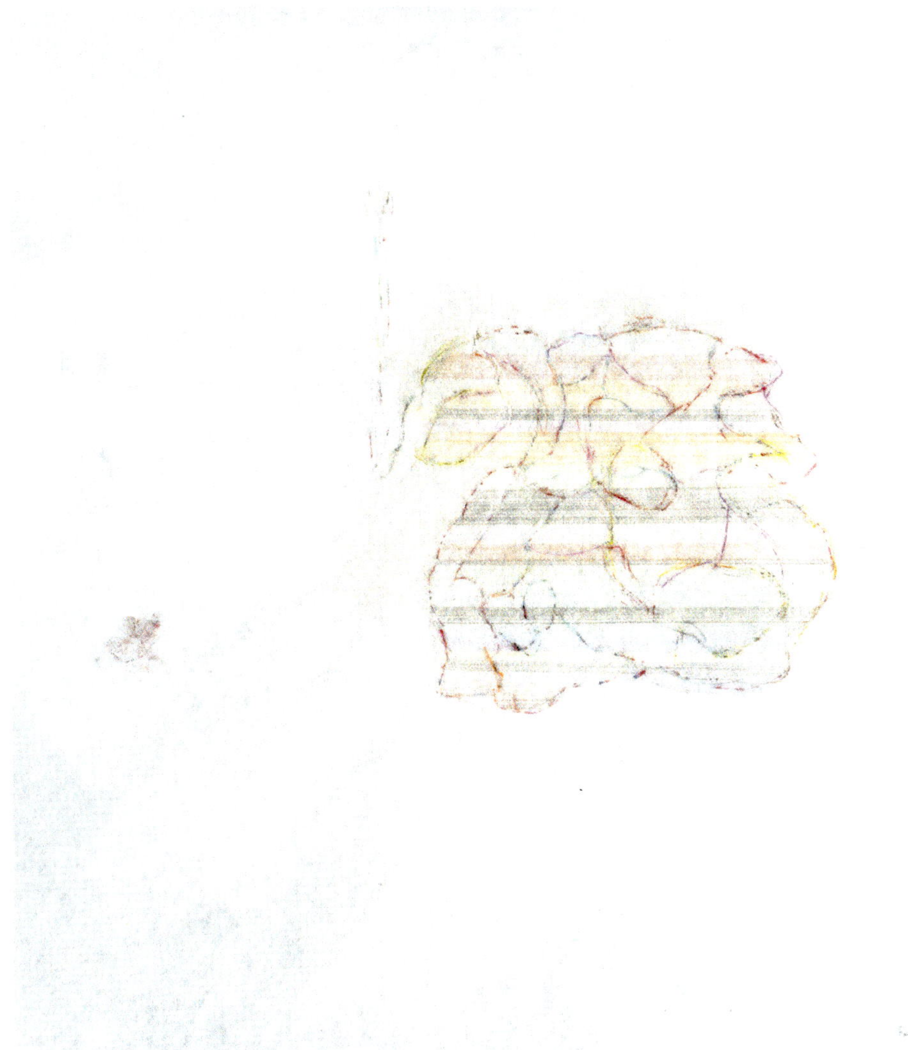

Twentieth Century Storm

Lightning the scythe
is cutting down the rain.
Swathes of water

fall like the clothes
- o the great coats for parting
  the great great coats
  that never returned!
fall like the clothes
of the far away
on the sky's empty field.

And in the grass of this rain
flowers
which grew with the strength of rivers
- o the pockets of the ferryman
  packed with the letters
  silences and promised numbers
  of those who left!
which grew with the strength of rivers
into estuaries.

Each flower began
in the palm of a hand,
each petal
in origin
a gesture an action
a touching.

Put your garden to my cheek
your five fingered garden
in another city
to my cheek.

The haycart
loaded with thunder
is trundling across the sky.

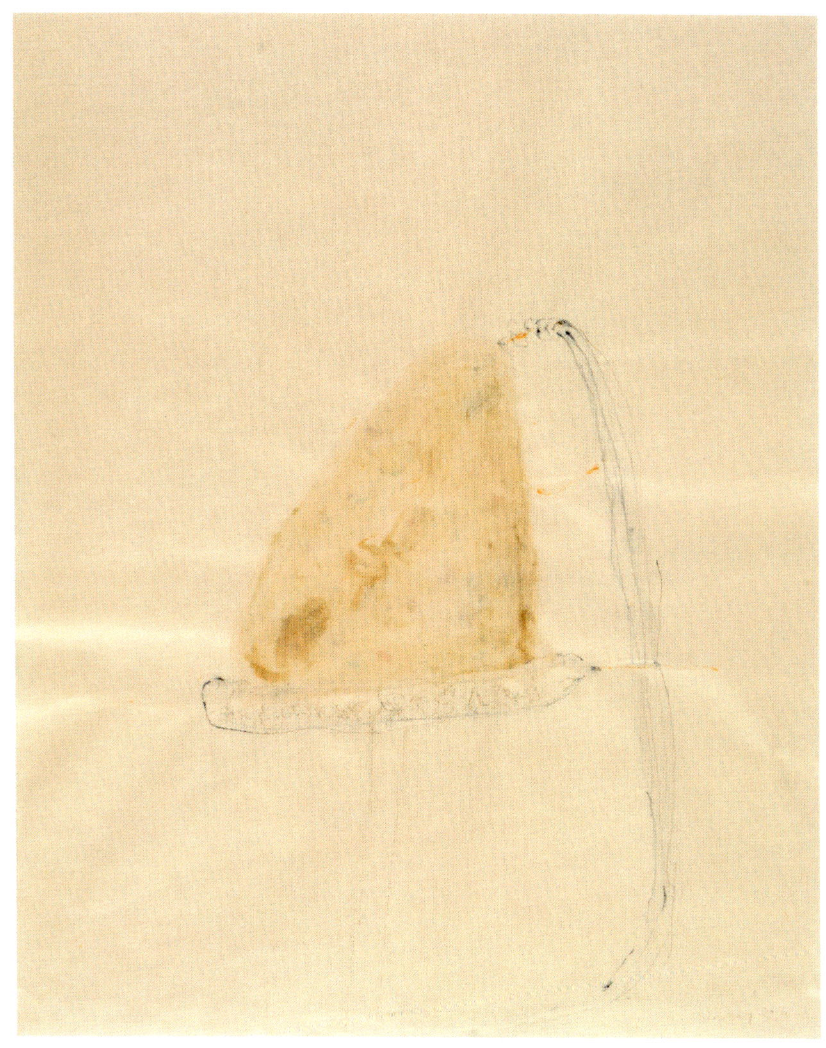

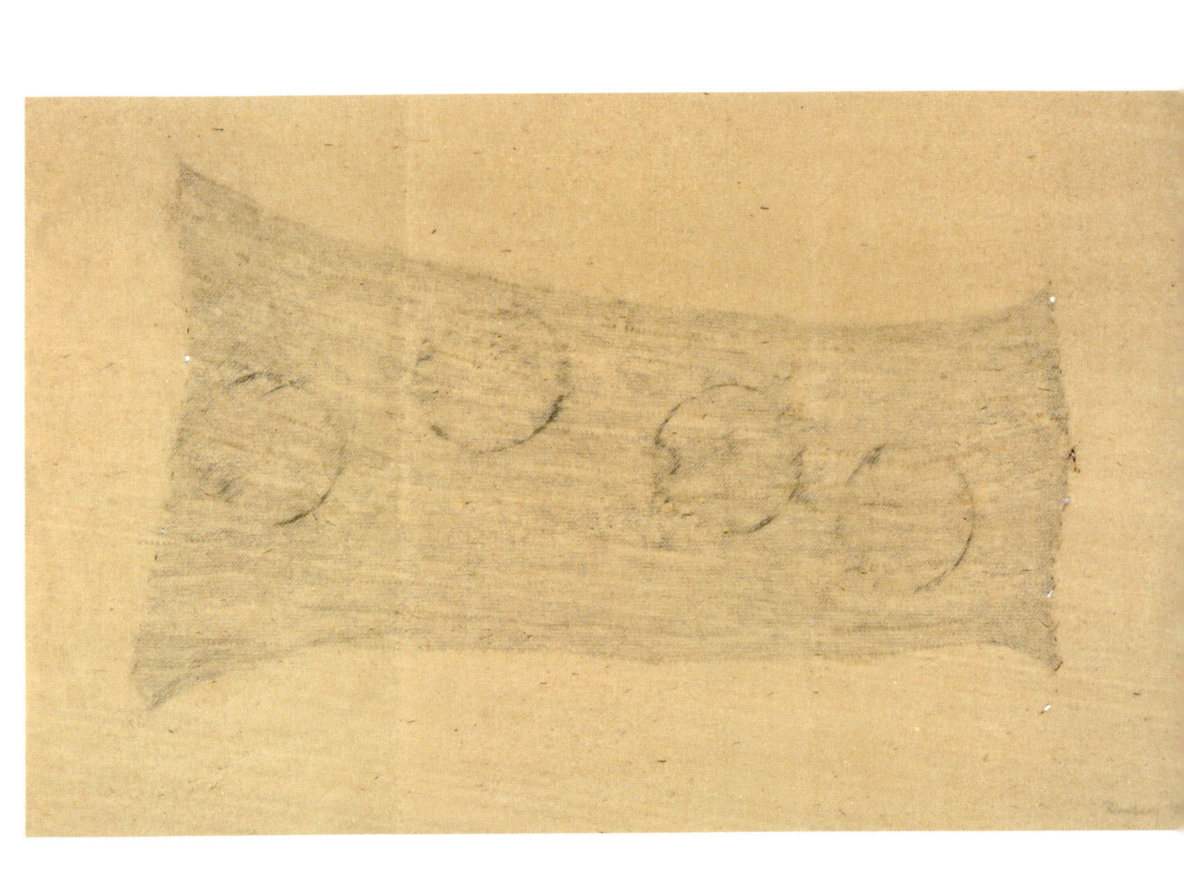

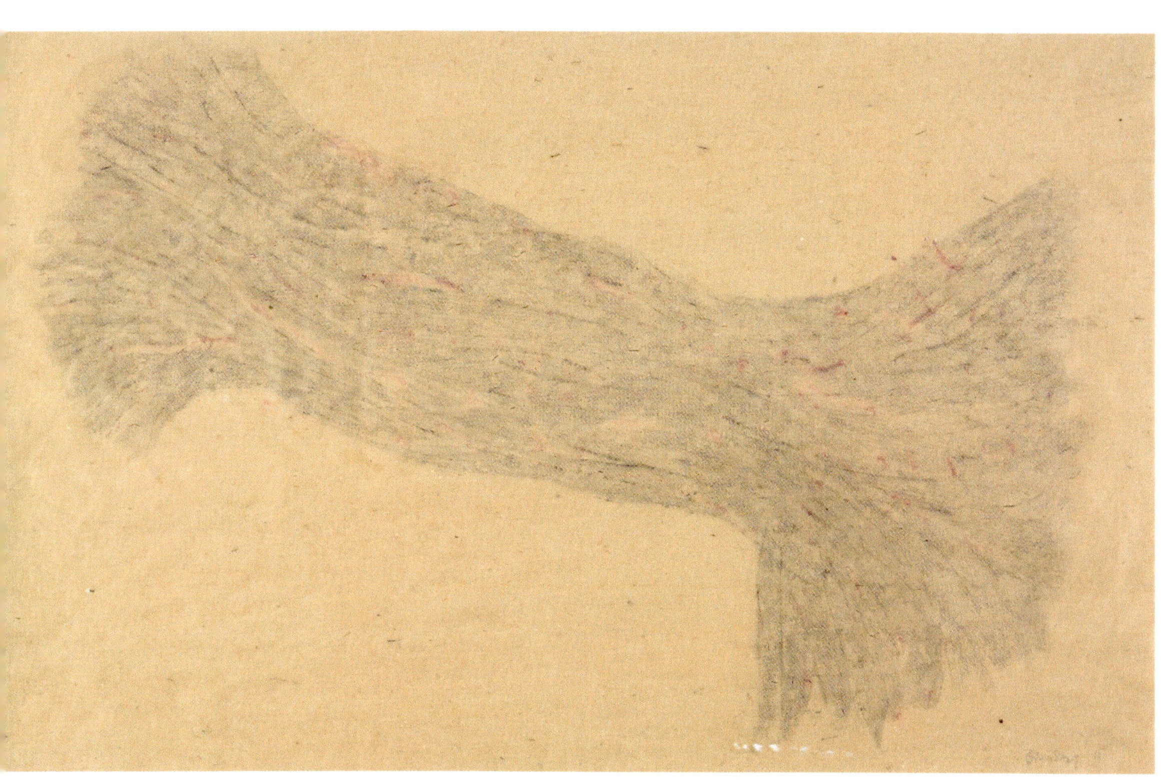

A butterfly disturbs a grain
The grain another
Till there is such friction in the dust
The sky spills its blue milk
On the stones that have conceived

A day is born

Forest

Each pine at dusk
lodges the bird
of its voice
perpendicular and still
the forest
indifferent to history
tearless as stone
repeats
in tremulous excitement
the ancient story
of the sun going down

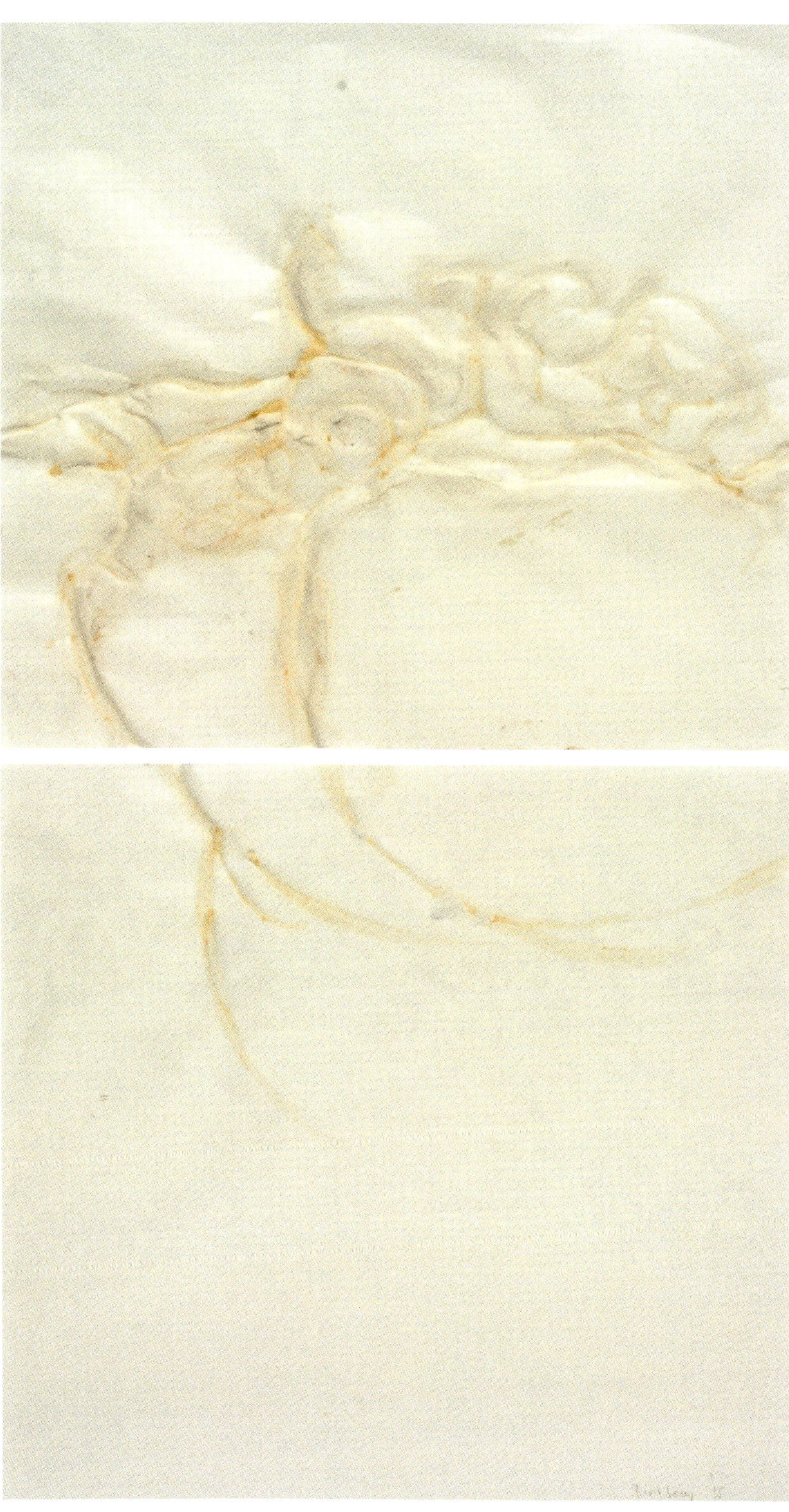

At Remaurian

V

Let the drawing stand up
And every dot
Yield a line
As the field that was sown
Is raised by its crop
And the nipple by the slow-growing tree.

Let the drawing stand up
And make of my legs
The legs of the table
On which this land is
Laid out like a towel
And placed like a bowel
Awaiting its water.

Let the drawing stand up
And its weight bear down
Till every line is opened
And the distance they cover
Is the format of the sky
Above my lover.

Let the drawing stand up
And pour from its lip
All that can turn my wheel.

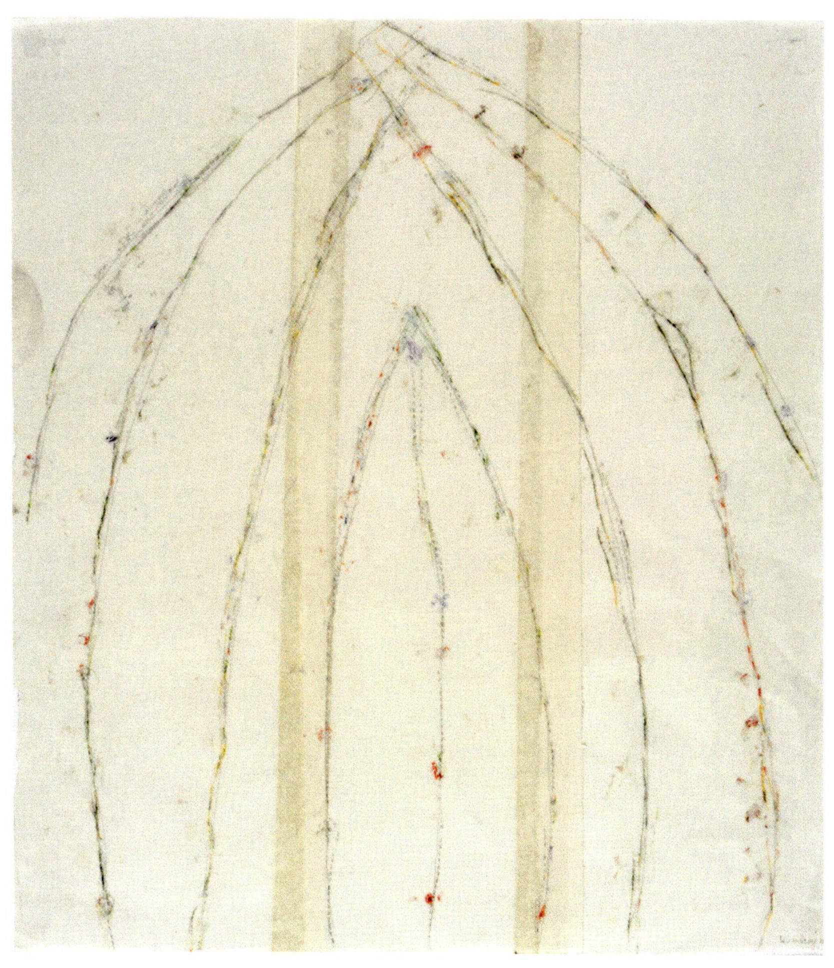

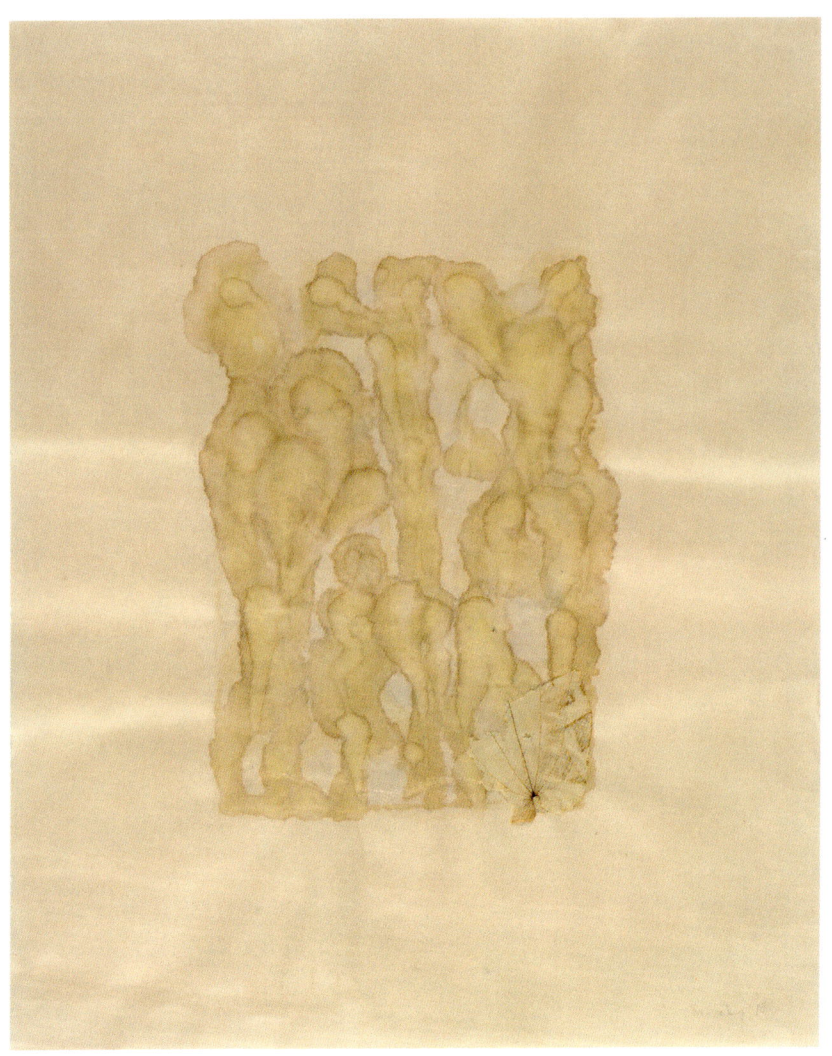

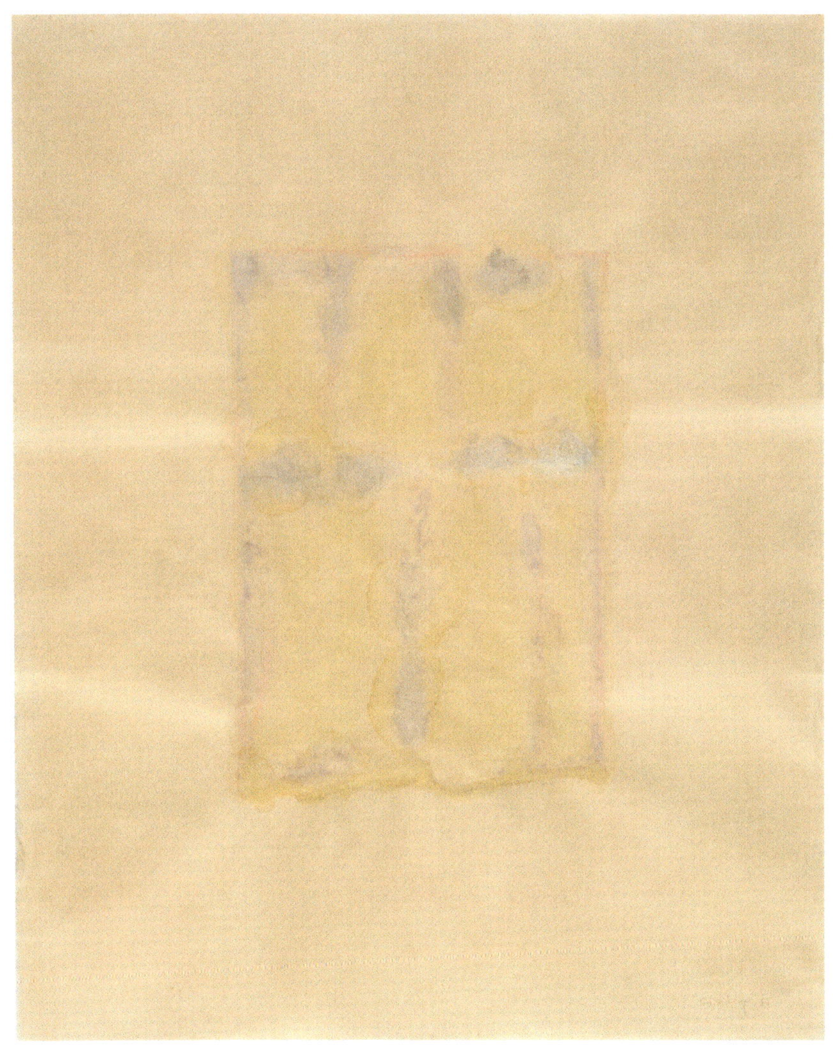

Pen Pencil and a Rubber

As I went home
on the suburban train
nothing in the world yet had an end
books to read
men´s tricks
the reaches of philosophy
Mother´s sewing
the KGB
and the things I could do to my hair

As I walked through the night
from the station
I made an inventory of what I was waiting for
a post as a teacher
next Sunday off
communism
a husband
my new winter coat
and poems not yet written

Before I undressed
and lay down in bed
I checked what I´d need next day
my notes on Hegel
a slice of koulibek
enough lined paper with a margin
seeds to feed the birds
pen pencil
and a rubber.

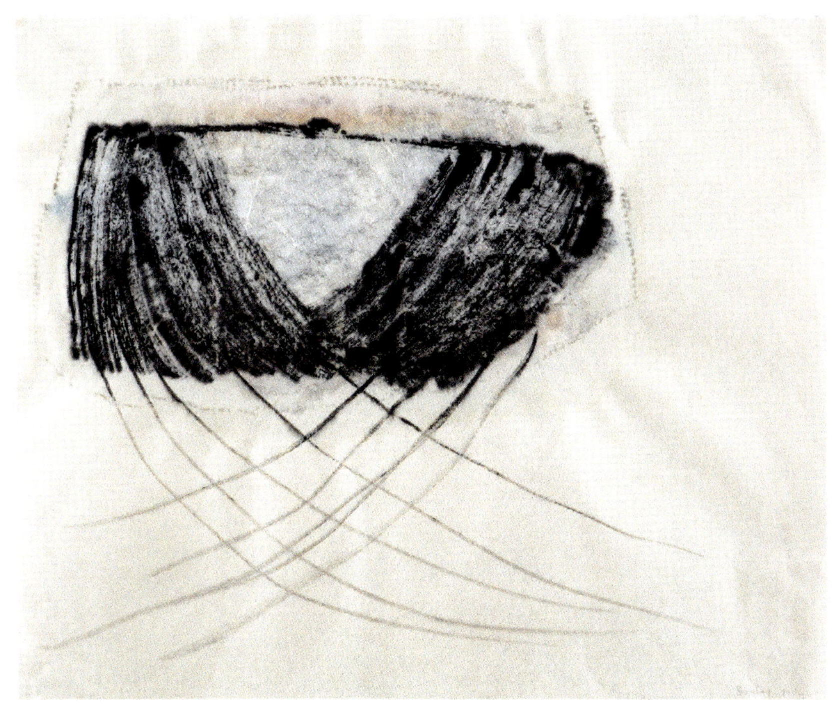

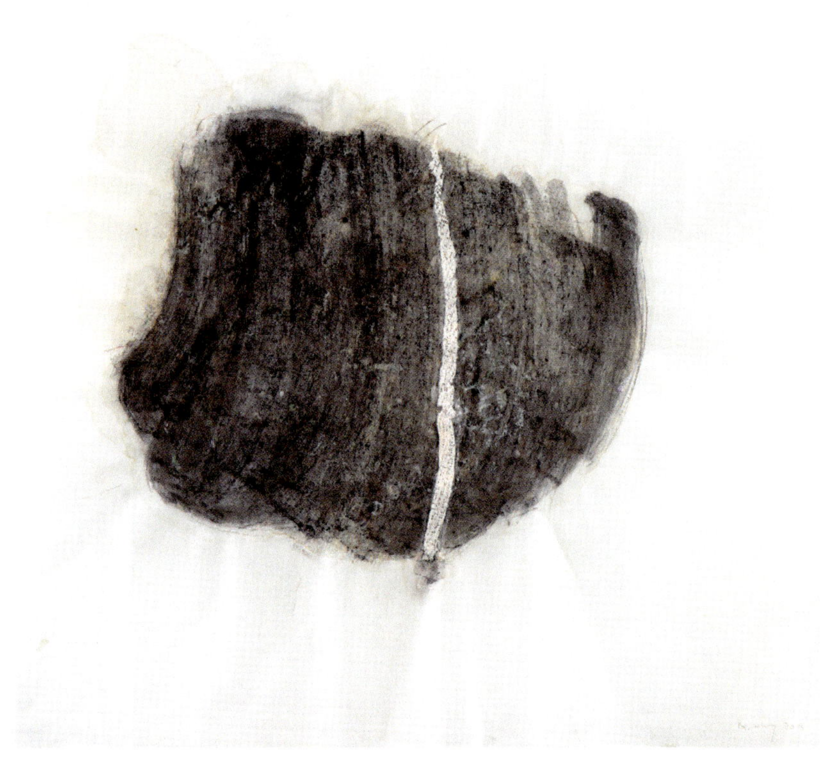

And our faces

When I open my wallet
to show my papers
pay money
or check the time of a train
I look at your face.

The flower´s pollen
is older than the mountains
Aravis is young
as mountains go.

The flower´s ovules
will be seeding still
when Aravis then aged
is no more than a hill.

The flower in the heart´s
wallet, the force
of what lives us
outliving the mountain.

And our faces, my heart, brief as photos.

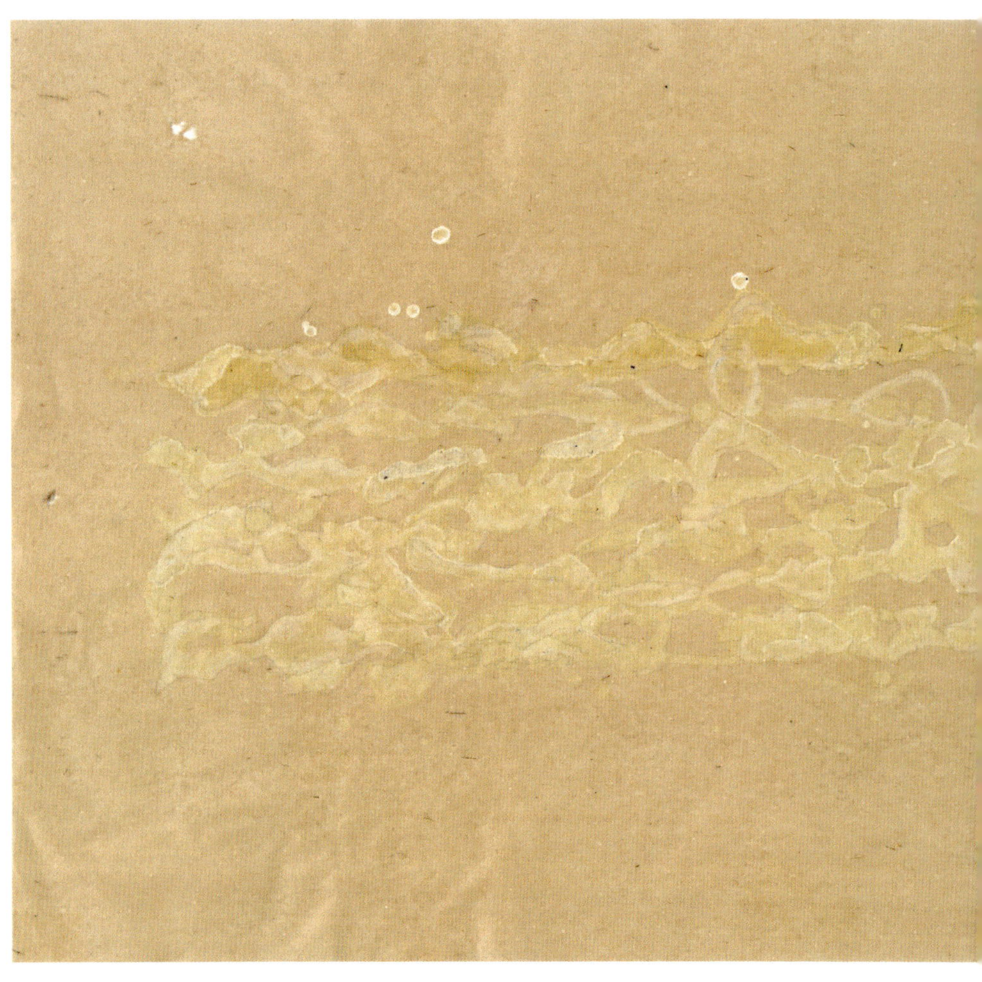

A day is born

Liane Birnberg

Malerin/ Komponistin
1948 in Bukarest geboren
Studierte Musik am Konservatorium
Leitete die erste Frauen-Popband in Osteuropa
Wurde Malerin und komponiert Neue Musik
Lebt und arbeitet in Berlin

Painter/Composer
1948 born in Bucharest
Studied Music at the Conservatory
Led the first Women's Popband in East Europe
Became a painter and composed new music
Lives and works in Berlin

John Berger

Autor
1926 in Stoke Newington geboren
Lebt und arbeitet in Frankreich
Schreibt Gedichte seit seinem 14. Lebensjahr
War einmal Maler
Verließ mit 16 die Schule
Hat immer noch eine Leidenschaft für Motorräder
Reueloser Marxist

Writer
1926 born in Stoke Newington
Lives and works in France
Wrote poems from age of 14 onwards
Was once a painter
Left school at 16
Still has a passion for motorbikes
Unrepentant Marxist

Bildernachweis

Seite 3: Stoffstärke, Abreibung, Farbstift auf Japanpapier, 42 x 60 cm
Seite 9: Abreibung und Seidenpapierfarbe auf Papier, 42 x 60 cm
Seite 11: Tusche auf Papier von John Berger
Seite 12: Collage, Büroklammern, Abreibung, Grafit auf Ovara Papier, 34 x 39 cm
Seite 13: Collage, Tusche, Grafit auf Reispapier, 50 x 50 cm
Seite 15: Abreibung, Granatapfel, Grafit auf Ovara Papier, 32 x 34 cm
Seite 17: Geschenkpapierfarbe, Abreibung auf Papier, 42 x 50 cm
Seite 19: Tusche, Abreibung, Geschenkpapierfarbe auf Maulbeerpapier, 15, 5 x 75,5 cm
Seite 20: Abreibung, Grafit, Silberfaden auf Maulbeerpapier, 19,5 x 75,5 cm
Seite 21: Abreibung, Grafit, Kreide, Brandlöcher auf Maulbeerpapier, 19,5 x 75,5 cm
Seite 24:Abreibung, Gips, Grafit auf Reispapier, 50 x 50 cm
Seite 27: Tusche, Geschenkpapierfarbe, Abreibung, Grafit auf Papier, 42 x 50 cm
Seite 28: Abreibung, Tusche auf Papier, 42 x 50 cm
Seite 29: Abreibung, Tusche auf Papier, 44 x 47 cm
Seite 31: Abreibung, Granatapfel, Bleistift auf Papier, 42 x 50 cm
Seite 33: Microglaskugeln, Stärke, Abreibung, Farbstift auf Reispapier, 50 x 50 cm
Seite 34: Ölkreide, Farbstift auf Reispapier, 50 x 50 cm
Seite 35: Abreibung, Farbstift auf Reispapier, 50 x 50 cm
Seite 37: Schellack, Abreibung, Bleistift, Tusche auf Papier, 42 x 50 cm
Seite 38: Tusche, Abreibung, Brandlöcher auf Maulbeerpapier, 19,5 x 75,5 cm
Seite 39: Abreibung, Grafit, Rotebeetesaft auf Maulbeerpapier, 19,5 x 75,5 cm
Seite 41: Abreibung, Stoffstärke auf Papier, je 32 x 34 cm
Seite 43: Abreibung, Farbstift auf drei Streifen Papier, 47,5 x 60 cm
Seite 44: Collage, Abreibung, Tee auf Papier, 42 x 50 cm
Seite 45: Abreibung, Tee auf Papier, 42 x 50 cm
Seite 47: Abreibung, Grafit, Pigment, Tusche auf Papier, 42 x 50 cm
Seite 48: Abreibung, Gips, Tusche auf Papier, 42 x 50 cm
Seite 50: Farbentferner, Bleistift auf Maulbeerpapier, 19,5 x 75,5 cm

Bibliografische Information der Deutschen Nationalbibliothek:
Die Deutsche Nationalbibliothek verzeichnet diese Publikation
in der Deutschen Nationalbibliografie; detaillierte bibliografische Daten
sind im Internet über http://www.d-nb.de abrufbar.

Bitte besuchen Sie auch **www.palmartpress.com**

ISBN: 978-3-941524-77-4

Auflage 500 Exemplare

Fotos: Jürgen Baumann, Uwe Steinert
Gedichte aus "John Berger Collected Poems", Smokestack Books, UK

PalmArtPress
Verlegerin: Catharine J. Nicely
Pfalzburgerstr. 69, 10719 Berlin

Druck: H. Heenemann GmbH & Co. KG, Berlin
Hergestellt in Deutschland

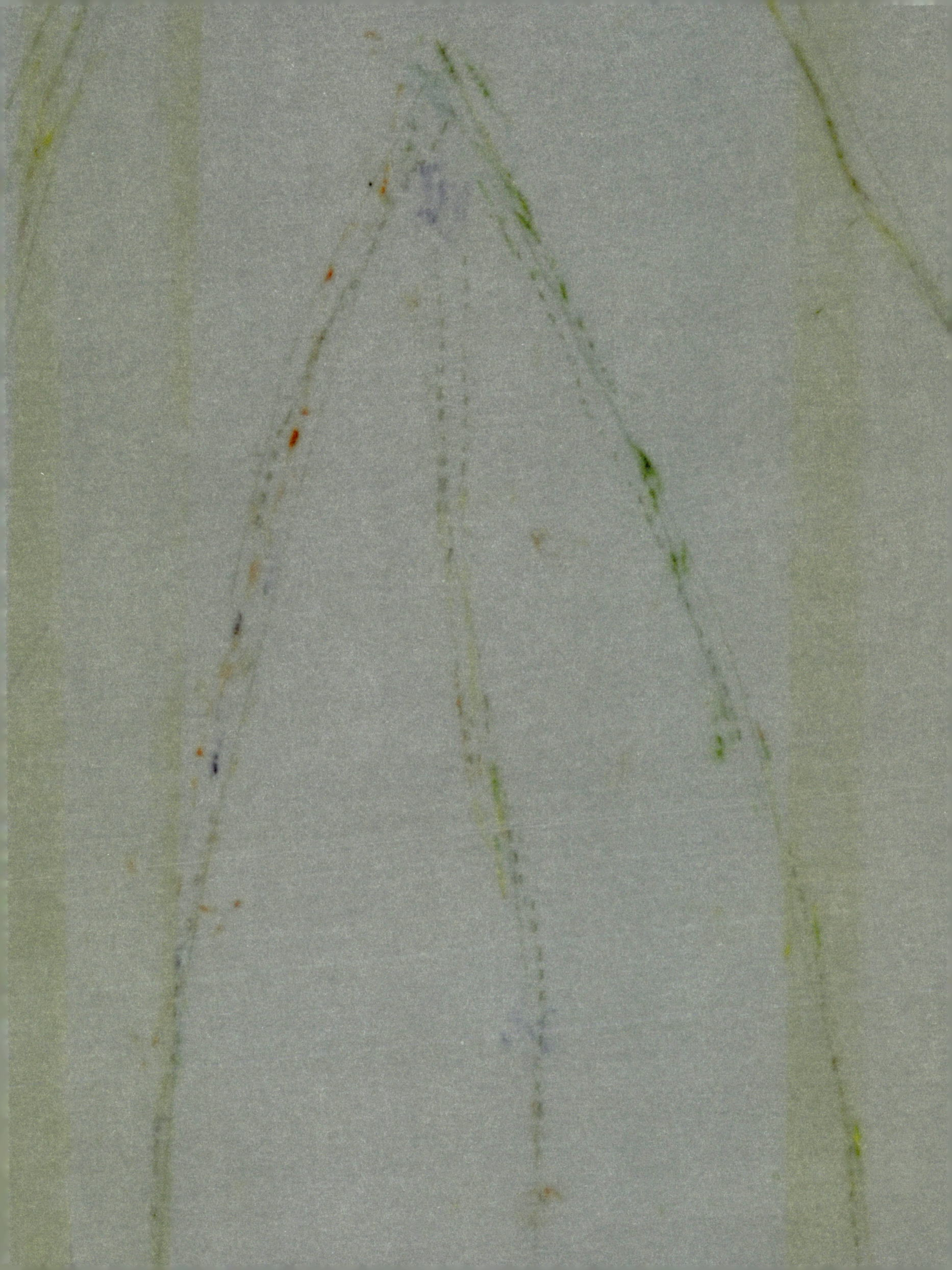

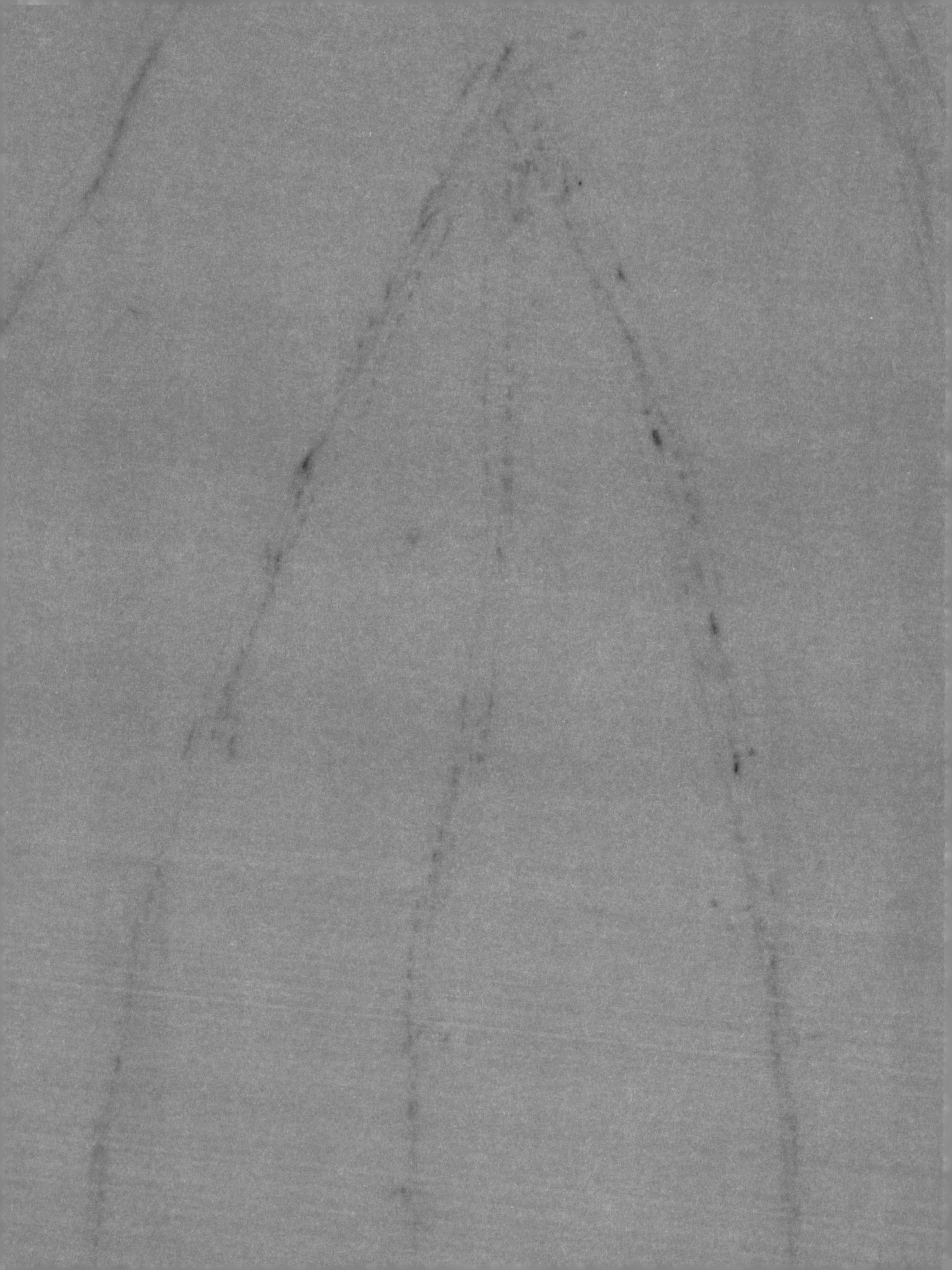